Published by RedDoor

www.reddoorpress.co.uk

© 2019 Sue Telford

The right of Sue Telford to be identified as author of this
Work has been asserted by her in accordance with sections
77 and 78 of the Copyright, Designs and Patents Act 1988

ISBN 978-1-913062-00-2

A CIP catalogue record for this book is available from the
British Library

Cocktail photographs: Amy Traynor
Step-by-step photographs: Sue Telford
Line illustrations: Joey Everett
Cover and internal design: sheerdesignandtypesetting.co.uk

Printed and bound in Poland by BZGraf S.A.

To Hein,
for his unwavering belief in this book

CONTENTS

INTRODUCTION

We are in the middle of a gin boom. By the time you have finished reading this book, there will probably be another two or three gins launched onto the market. At the last count, there were well over 5000 different gins produced globally. And while this is fantastic news for all you gin lovers, it means there's a dizzying array of choice out there.

How to Drink Gin was written to demystify some of the 'fluff' that currently surrounds gin. It offers you practical help to make better choices in bars, online, in the supermarket and at home when buying or serving gin or anything gin related.

Most of the published gin books out there are about the history of gin. As good as they are, they don't cater to the fledgling gin enthusiast or someone with a knowledge of gin but a thirst for more practical help. There are snippets of gin history in this book too, but hopefully not too many to overwhelm its general purpose – which is to be useful both to those of you out there who know their juniper berries when it comes to gin and those of you who have just started out on their journey of discovery.

By the end of the book, you will have discovered how gin is crafted, genned up on the key botanicals used in gin and learned how to 'taste' gin with confidence. You will have built up a go-to gin cabinet, gathered together some basic bar tools, be creative in your choice of mixer, experimented with creating some simple but effective gin garnishes, and mastered a menu of classic gin cocktails to whip up at a moment's notice and impress everyone with your mixology skills.

My aim is to make gin culture and cocktails accessible and fun. Join me on my gin journey to become a fully fledged ginthusiast.

CHAPTER 1

SO WHAT EXACTLY IS GIN?

This chapter outlines the current definition of gin, how it differs from vodka and whisky, and the different methods used to make gin. It includes a brief summary of the different styles – from London Dry to new contemporary.

THE DEFINITION OF GIN

The current definition of gin is that it is a spirit whose main flavour must be juniper berry and it has to be bottled at no less than 37.5% ABV.

While this might seem perfectly straightforward it is not always as simple as that. EU regulations as of 2019 have changed and they were meant to tighten up the definition of gin. But that doesn't seem to have been the case. You might want to pour yourself a large G&T for this chapter.

ABV

ABV is the abbreviation for 'alcohol by volume' and is an indicator of how strong the spirit is. It literally means the percentage of alcohol at 100% strength in the total volume of liquid. For instance, 100ml of spirit at 40% would contain 40ml of 100% strength alcohol. All gins will be marked with their ABV on the label. Most craft gins hover around the 40 to 43%

mark. Some more commercial gins will be at 37.5% ABV, the lowest they can legally go and stay within the legal framework for a spirit.

ETHANOL – THE BASE OF ALL SPIRITS

Whisky, rum and vodka all start out in life, like gin, as ethanol. Whisky may be distilled from barley, rum from sugar cane or molasses, and vodka from just about anything really that contains sugar or starch. But the result is pretty much the same: ethanol. The flavour of the base spirit is affected by the grain or molasses used. In the case of triple-distilled vodka, there shouldn't be any taste at all. In the distilling industry, this ethanol is called neutral grain spirit, or NGS.

The clue is in the term 'neutral'. The base for gin must be as neutral as possible for what comes afterwards. It is how this neutral grain spirit is treated which makes gin.

While whisky ethanol is stored in barrels or casks for a minimum of three years before it can be called whisky, and rum ethanol is either bottled immediately, sometimes spiced or aged in casks, and vodka left pretty much well alone, gin has various flavourings added to it. The predominant flavouring is the juniper berry.

THE BOTANICALS OR FLAVOURINGS

The gin distiller takes the NGS and adds flavouring
to it in the form of botanicals. Botanicals can be
any edible herb, spice, fruit, flower, seed or nut that
you can think of. They are what make the creation
of gin so exciting. Like cooking, the skill of a master
distiller is like that of a great chef. We will look into
botanicals in more detail in Chapter 2.

COMPOUND VS DISTILLED

Now that the distiller has assembled the NGS and
botanicals, they can choose to either make gin using
the cold compound method or distillation.

Cold compounding, or more commonly just
compounding gin, means steeping the botanicals in the
NGS without any form of heat added. The NGS can
be any strength but is often around the required ABV
of the finished product. The botanicals can be left for
hours or days until the distiller is satisfied that the gin
is finished, then they are filtered out. Compound gin,
or bathtub gin as it is also known (see page 10), usually
takes on a certain amount of colour from the botanicals.

Unfortunately compound gin has a bad reputation
due some gins being nothing more than ethanol

with flavourings or essences added. As long as the main flavouring is juniper they can still legally be called gin. These gins should be, but are not, labelled clearly so as not to deceive.

Distilling is when heat is applied to the botanicals, which causes them to give up their flavour. If the distiller chooses to distil their gin then the NGS is put into a still at around 40 to 55% ABV. A distiller may favour a particular type of still from the traditional pot still to a column still.

Usually, the botanicals are added at this point and either left to macerate for a number of hours in the NGS, in a process called steeping, before extraction takes place by distillation. Or distillation can take place immediately. Usually, the former is preferred, to gain maximum flavour.

Another form of distillation is vapour extraction. The botanicals are suspended in a basket above the steam from the still and extraction takes place by steam distillation. Sometimes the botanicals are vapour-distilled individually, or in varying combinations, then blended afterwards.

There is another method, which is a combination of distillation and compounding, when the distilled gin has more botanicals added to it, post-distillation. These infused gins are very popular right now.

THE WATER

Once distilled, the gin will be roughly 80 to 95% ABV and has to be diluted with water to bring the ABV down to a strength of around 40%. Compound gin often doesn't need any dilution.

STYLES OF GIN

There are various styles of gin on the market. This list is not exhaustive but the ones you are most likely to encounter are:

Distilled Gin ~ is your regular gin, if you like. Distilled to at least 96% with juniper predominant and bottled at no less than 37.5%. If it contains less than 0.1g sweetening per litre of finished gin you can add the word 'dry' to the label.

London Dry Gin ~ like dry distilled gin it doesn't contain more sweetening than 0.1g to earn the title 'dry'. London Dry Gin was once a gin distilled in one shot. i.e. a kind of all-in-one method with the NGS and botanicals added at the beginning of the distillation and nothing is added afterwards and no blending takes place. New EU laws have changed all that. Now a London Dry can be made of blended distillates as long as they are all made using the London Dry one shot method. I told you you would need a large G&T. London Dry gins make great cocktail gins as long as their botanical profile isn't too strong.

Compound or 'Bathtub' Gin ~ the gin is made by steeping the botanicals and filtering, as described on page 7. Compounds gins usually have a faint straw colour picked up from the botanicals.

Contemporary Gin ~ light on juniper and big on other flavours, contemporary gins are pushing the boundaries as to what gin actually is. Some of the controversy surrounding gin right now relates to contemporary gins not having enough juniper in them to be technically real gins but rather flavoured vodkas jumping on the gin bandwagon.

Infused Gin ~ a base gin is distilled then infused post-distillation, as described on page 8. Often the infusion is one of fruit to add complexity, flavour and weight to a fruity gin.

Cask-aged Gin ~ the gin is first distilled then aged in a cask like whisky. Unlike whisky, the gin isn't usually left for three years, more likely a matter of weeks or months. Just long enough for the gin to absorb the flavour of the cask, be it a former sherry, whisky or bourbon cask. Cask-aged gins have a smokiness and sweetness about them and usually a slight coloration.

Old Tom Gin ~ a sweet style of gin popular during the nineteenth century, now coming back into fashion where a sweetening agent, such as sugar or honey, is added during and post-distillation. Often sipped neat or used as the base spirit in a Tom Collins (see page 58).

Navy Strength Gin ~ gin that is at least 57% ABV, it gets its name from the Royal Navy. It is said that in the past gin drunk by Navy officers had to be at least 57% ABV so that if during stormy weather the gin barrel broke and drenched the gunpowder, it would be left unaffected and still ignite. A gin with less alcohol, on the other hand, would wet the gunpowder and cause it to be unusable.

Another story is that suspicious sailors would want proof that their rations were strong enough. Without hydrometers, which measure the alcohol strength in a liquid, they mixed their ration with gunpowder and set fire to it. Only a liquid at 57% ABV would catch fire, (or explode), as to satisfy suspicious sailors. The only problem with this theory is that the ratings drank rum and the officers gin. Either way, whether this is true or not, the name stuck and now this style of gin is seeing a resurgence. The botanicals are often more robust, too, to withstand the higher alcohol content.

Craft Gin ~ a fairly meaningless term that seems nevertheless to be used quite a lot, along with the term 'artisan' and 'small-batch'. All gins, even in large commercial distilleries, are crafted. The craft comes from the skill of the distiller.

Juniper-flavoured Spirit Drink (EU wording not mine) ~ you are legally allowed to create a 'juniper-flavoured spirit drink' by flavouring ethanol with juniper and watering it down to as low as 30%. This is not gin.

Gin Liqueur ~ the new EU laws allow the terms gin and liqueur to be combined as long as the predominant flavour is gin i.e. juniper, contains 100g sweetening per litre of finished product and is above 15% ABV.

GIN HISTORY IN SNIPPETS

ITALIAN MONKS

From medieval herbal tonic to modern-day global spirit, gin has had a long and fascinating history.

11thC ~ It is believed that Italian monks were flavouring crude spirits with juniper berries as long ago as the Middle Ages. With the tradition dating from Roman times of using juniper berries in medicine as a cure for a wide range of ailments, including indigestion, and the fact that *Juniperus communis* was growing on the monks' doorstep in abundance (some of the finest, sweetest juniper berries still grow in Italy), together with the fact that monks everywhere seem to make a hobby out of brewing and distilling, it would be no big surprise if the rumour were true: that the origin of gin lies deep within the Italian countryside.

CHAPTER 2

KNOW YOUR BOTANICALS

A botanical is a term for a herb, flower, spice or root that can be used to flavour gin. It is the organic compounds contained within these botanicals that are the flavour powerhouses prized by distillers. There are hundreds of potential botanicals and it is the master distiller's skill in combining these that gives gin its varied complexity. No two gin recipes are ever the same.

This chapter covers ten key botanicals most commonly found in gin: juniper, coriander seed, angelica root, orris root, cassia bark, cardamom, liquorice root, lavender, grains of paradise and citrus. Each botanical will be discussed in detail as well as its botanical name, plant family, range and the parts of the plant used in the making of gin.

COMMON JUNIPER

Botanical name: *Juniperus communis*
Plant family: Cupressaceae
Range: widespread across the northern hemisphere
Parts used: the berries, or more properly 'cones'

Details: It makes sense to start with juniper. Juniper berries are the main flavouring for gin – as you are probably aware by now!

Juniper is the low-growing, shrubby evergreen conifer on which the juniper 'berries' grow. Like other members of the cypress family, it has small needle-like leaves. Its favoured habitat is chalk downland, moorland, coastal dunes, rocky hillsides and the understorey of coniferous woodland.

The trees are dioecious, meaning that the conifers either have male or female flowers. This makes things a bit tricky when it comes to pollination, as the female flowers are pollinated by wind. The berries take up to two years to fully ripen from green to a beautiful deep purply-bluey-brown. When ripe, the berries are eaten by birds and so the seeds hidden within are dispersed.

Packed with bioflavonoids and antioxidants with antibacterial and antifungal properties juniper berries are truly a superfood, but only recently have the health benefits begun to be understood. There are several claims surrounding juniper: it is professed to have natural antiseptic properties, an ability to reduce blood pressure and act as an aid to digestion.

In gin production, the majority of juniper berries are sourced from around the Mediterranean, with the finest berries growing in Italy and Macedonia. Juniper berries typically form half to two-thirds of the total botanicals in a batch of gin. The dried berries (not fresh) can be crushed or left whole to macerate in neutral grain spirit to release their unique flavours before distillation.

Bite into a juniper berry and you will get a powerful complex hit of resinous, piney, lemony, bittersweet flavour. The flesh of the berry is sweet, with the real juniper kick being in the seeds. The main flavour compounds are alpha-pinene, responsible for the pine notes and limonene, which is as its name suggests, citrus. Both these compounds pop up in other common gin botanicals. The complexity of the organic compounds is what makes the creation of gin so interesting. Juniper is the Queen of Botanicals.

CORIANDER SEED

Botanical name: *Coriandrum sativum*
Plant family: Apiaceae (carrot)
Range: southern Mediterranean, Asia and North Africa
Parts used: typically the seeds, but the leaves too can be used

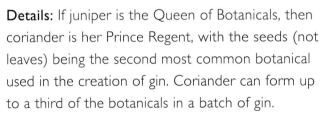

Details: If juniper is the Queen of Botanicals, then coriander is her Prince Regent, with the seeds (not leaves) being the second most common botanical used in the creation of gin. Coriander can form up to a third of the botanicals in a batch of gin.

From medicine to cooking, coriander has been used for millennia. Coriander seeds dating back to

6000 BC have been found in a Neolithic cave in Israel; Tutankhamun was rather partial to coriander, as evidenced by the number of baskets of seeds found in his tomb.

Romans, those culinary wanderers, took coriander seed with them all over their empire, dropping it willy-nilly for archaeologists to discover hundreds of years later. Indeed, Roman gourmet foodie Apicius used the leaves and seeds in many of his recipes. Interestingly, the Greeks likened the smell of coriander leaves to that of bedbugs. The name coriander is believed to stem from the Greek for bug: *koris* (cori).

Coriander is an annual with a long taproot, easy to grow in warmer climes but difficult in cooler conditions. It is the seeds gin distillers are mostly interested in. Seeds vary in flavour and pungency from region to region, according to the varying levels of heat, sunshine and soil components found in different parts of the world.

Juniper and coriander share the volatile oil linalool, which goes some way to explaining why they make such good companions. Alpha-pinene (pine) and gamma-Terpinene (lemon) are also present in coriander, giving the seeds a citrusy, spicy, woody twang. Try putting a whole coriander seed in your mouth, then bite down on it as you take a sip of your favourite London Dry. You get a real spicy, lemony hit.

ANGELICA ROOT

Botanical name: *Angelica archangelica*
Plant family: Apiaceae (carrot)
Range: widespread across the northern
hemisphere
Parts used: mainly the roots, but the stem can also
be used

Details: Angelica root is the Cinderella of the
botanical theatre, yet it is a key botanical in the
making of gin. And while juniper and coriander
aren't exactly the Ugly Sisters, they tend to get
the invitations to the ball, while angelica root
is often overlooked. Yet the vast majority of
gins include every member of this trio. Joanne
Moore of G&J Distillers describes them as the
'Holy Trinity'.

The name *Angelica archangelica* comes from the
Greek *arkangelos*, or archangel, perhaps because it
blooms on St Michael's (the Archangel) Day. It is
said that St Michael prescribed it as a medicine for
the plague.

Known since the twelfth century for its health
benefits, wild angelica contains stimulating
properties for the lungs and is used as a relief for
lung congestion. It is also used as an aid to digestion.

Angelica is a member of the plant family that includes parsley, carrot and celery. Wild angelica is widespread in Northern Europe and is found as far north as Greenland. It prefers to grow in damp soil in the shade near running water and can grow to approximately 2.5 metres in height. Its inconspicuous flowers form umbellifers, like umbrellas. Commercially grown in Europe, angelica from Saxony, Germany is said to be the best.

Like juniper and coriander, angelica contains alpha-pinene. In fact, it has more than eighty different aroma compounds, including cyclopentadecanolide. This compound is present in the roots in tiny amounts, less than 1%, but even this minuscule amount gives the roots a musky aroma.

All of the plant can be used: seeds, the hollow hexagonal stems and the roots. The stems are often candied and used in confectionery and cakes. The roots are fleshy and long and have to be harvested before autumn in their first year of growth before they can be invaded by insects. They are dried soon after harvesting.

In the production of gin, the roots are believed to be a fixative for the other botanicals. The dried-out root smells rather like damp cardboard. The distilled taste is rather strange, definitely savoury or umami; it has been described as mushroom-like.

ORRIS ROOT

Botanical names: *Iris germanica, Iris pallida, Iris florentina*

Plant family: Iridaceae

Range: the Mediterranean, Morocco, China and India

Parts used: the root

Details: Orris root is one of the more expensive and popular botanicals used in the production of gin. Long prized as a fixative in the perfume industry, it is believed to have the same qualities in the distilling of gin, binding and fixing all the various flavours together.

The root, or more properly rhizome, comes from the herbaceous perennial iris plant. Once the rhizome is harvested it is dried out for up to five years in a process of oxidation before being ground down to a powder. It is this drying period that allows the essential oils contained within the root to oxidise and degrade to give the root its characteristic violet aroma. It is this powder that goes into the still.

Orris root has a delicately sweet, earthy, floral aroma and taste when distilled on its own. You would think it would be knocked out by the more boisterous botanicals. Yet despite its shy, retiring nature orris root seems to have the ability to bring all the more extrovert botanicals in gin to a harmonious conclusion. Hence its popularity among distillers.

CASSIA BARK

Botanical name: *Cinnamomum cassia*
Plant family: Lauraceae
Range: South East Asia and China
Parts used: the bark

Details: Ever taken a sip of gin to detect an elusive spicy, clove-like flavour hovering around at the finish? Chances are you are enjoying the fragrant delights of *Cinnamomum cassia*. More commonly known as Chinese cinnamon.

Cassia bark is the big cousin of cinnamon: earthy and pungent compared to the lighter, brighter notes of cinnamon, and stronger with a clove-like punch. Cassia is a bit of a bruiser and comes in thick pieces of bark, difficult to grind into a powder. Cinnamon, by contrast, comes in delicate thin quills, easily ground down to a fine powder.

Chinese cassia is an evergreen shrubby tree that grows ten to fifteen metres tall. It thrives in South

East Asia and China. There are several subspecies, but *Cinnamomum cassia* or *Cinnamomum aromaticum* is the most commonly used. As a member of the plant family Lauraceae, its leaves are long and pinnate like a laurel. The flowers are white with yellow stamens. But it is the bark gin distillers are interested in.

Cassia bark (and cinnamon) contain the organic compound cinnamaldehyde, which gives both of them that distinctive aroma and taste. Used as a flavouring in chewing gum, confectionery, baking and seasoning meat and fish, it is also known as an effective mosquito repellent.

Mentioned as far back as 2,700 BC in the agricultural and medicinal book *Pen Ts'ao Ching*, cassia was grouped as one of the 'noble herbs' in Chinese medicine, known for their stimulating properties. In *Ebers Papyrus*, the Egyptian medical papyrus, dating to 1,550 BC cassia also gets a mention.

Modern medicine, however, doesn't recognise any health benefits of taking cinnamon or cassia supplements. Ingested in large amounts cassia can actually be quite dangerous. It contains a substance called coumarin which can cause liver damage, but this would have to be taken in excessive amounts.

Cassia is added to the gin still as crushed pieces. It provides a nice spicy, warming, earthy finish to gin and when used adds complexity and dimension to the flavour profile.

CARDAMOM

Botanical name: *Elettaria cardamomum*
Plant family: Zingiberaceae
Range: widespread, from India and Nepal to Vietnam, Cambodia, Thailand, Central America and Tanzania
Parts used: the seeds and seedpods

Details: Once tasted, cardamom is never forgotten and deserves its reputation as being the Queen of Spices. Cardamom is quoted as being the third most expensive spice in the world after saffron and vanilla, due to its labour-intensive harvesting. Every pod is picked by hand.

The cousin of cardamom is *Elettaria ensal* or Wild Sri Lankan cardamom but this is chemically different from true cardamom. Black cardamom, *Amomum subulatum*, a native of northeastern India, is different again. It has a coarser smoky aroma and flavour.

Once traded along the Spice Route, cardamom
has long been prized. Used as a perfume by the
Greeks and Romans, it rates a mention in fourth
century BC Sanskrit texts where it was described as
being given as an offering. It was also taken by the
Vikings to Scandinavia, where it is still very popular,
particularly as a flavouring in baking. Indeed, it is still
used in Scandinavian gingerbread today.

Until 1980 India was the world's largest grower
of cardamom, where it originated along the Malabar
Coast, or the Western Ghats, a hilly region known
as the Cardamom Hills. Today it also grows in
Nepal, Sri Lanka, Vietnam, Cambodia, Thailand,
Tanzania and Central America, where Guatemala
has taken the lead.

Cardamom is a clump-forming herbaceous
perennial with long dagger-like leaves that grow
from rhizomes to up to six metres in height. Its
habitat is the forest floor and to mimic this, growers
often intercrop it with tea, betel nut palms or black
pepper. It flowers year round with white to lilac
flower spikes that grow up to a metre long and are
pollinated by insects. The ridged green torpedo-
shaped pods, the carriers, contain the black seeds,
where most of the aroma and flavour is to be found.
The pods are harvested every three to five weeks
when ripe and before they have the chance to split

and spill their precious cargo. Drying in a curing room, in a method known as flue curing, keeps the green colour of the pods.

The seed oil has antibacterial properties, which have been used to preserve meat. It is also frequently used in curry and to flavour masala chai, and to flavour the Arabic drink of *gahwa*, a cardamom-spiced coffee. Used in Ayurvedic medicine, cardamom has a whole host of uses: commonly used to treat stomach ailments, asthma, colds, sore throats, bronchitis, heart problems, stress, overwork, depression, eyesight problems, as a skin conditioner and for bad breath.

The aroma is a spicy floral herbal bergamot with hints of lavender and lime and in gin it has a spicy perfumed taste that you will notice is quite distinctive, once your taste buds are attuned.

LIQUORICE ROOT

Botanical name: *Glycyrrhiza glabra*
Plant family: Leguminosae
Range: widespread across the Middle East and southeastern Europe
Parts used: the root

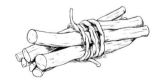

Details: Surprisingly, liquorice is a member of the pea family. The botanical name comes from the Greek 'glukus' and 'rhiza', meaning 'sweet root'. And this would sum up this plant with its aniseed-flavoured roots.

Grown in the UK since the sixteenth century, it was cultivated by Dominican monks in the town of Pontefract, home of Pontefract cakes, forerunners of Liquorice Allsorts. But the Egyptians were already using it centuries earlier to make a kind of tea from the leaves to cure many ailments. Liquorice root is said to have many medicinal benefits, including the anti-inflammatory ability to soothe an upset stomach.

Popular today as a sweet flavouring in the Netherlands, it is eaten as *zoute drop* or salty liquorice. The bare unadulterated root of liquorice is chewed in Italy, France and Spain.

The plant grows to over 1 metre tall, but it is the root gin distillers are interested in for its aniseed flavour, due to the organic compound anethole. The rhizomes are harvested every three to five years then dried before being crushed to a powder or chopped into small pieces.

Distilled with a light hand in gin liquorice root can add weight and a certain spiciness. Too much and you have a gin that tastes of the sweets liquorice torpedoes.

LAVENDER

Botanical name: *Lavandula angustifolia*
(English lavender)
Plant family: Lamiaceae
Range: Europe, China and southeast India
Parts used: the flowers

Details: Easy to grow and drought tolerant, lavender is a decorative woody shrub grown for its fragrant violet-coloured flowers. The plant is found widespread across Europe, particularly favouring the Mediterranean sunshine. As a member of the mint family, lavender also has its culinary uses, most commonly in baking. It is the flowers most bakers and cooks are interested in, not the leaves.

This versatile flower is also used for its anti-inflammatory and antiseptic properties in the commercial production of lavender oil. It has long been believed that lavender fragrance has calming qualities, hence its use in perfuming bath products. Lavender honey is also sought after.

Lavender might seem like a strange botanical to find in gin, but its flowers are popular among distillers for their floral yet slightly resinous and camphor-like flavour with a hint of citrus. Used with care, it adds complexity and 'lifts' the gin.

GRAINS OF PARADISE

Botanical name: *Aframomum melegueta*

Plant family: Zingiberaceae

Range: West Africa

Parts used: the seeds

Details: A perennial herb and part of the ginger family, the *Aframomum melegueta* favours swampy marsh-like areas and can grow to 1.5 metres tall. It has long, narrow palm-like leaves and purple flowers that go on to form fruits containing the glossy brown little seeds known as grains of paradise. The seeds go by a number of names, with the most common being Guinea pepper, which gives some indication of the aromatic peppery nature of these seeds.

In the fourteenth and fifteenth centuries, the seeds were used as a cheap substitute for the more expensive black pepper. Traders named them grains of paradise to bump up their value, claiming they were grown in the Garden of Eden. Today the roles of the two spices have been reversed and black pepper is much more inexpensive.

In African folk medicine, these little seeds are used both as an anti-inflammatory cure for stomach problems and as an aphrodisiac. The flavour is peppery but not as coarse or strong as black pepper, pleasantly floral and with a soft citrus taste. Not surprisingly, these seeds are widely used in cooking where they are sometimes referred to as 'gourmet pepper'.

In gin, they impart a sophisticated spicy flavour that complements the citrus elements in juniper very well, adding complexity to the botanical profile.

CITRUS

Botanical names: *many Citrus species*
Plant family: Rutaceae
Range: widespread, tropical and subtropical, the Mediterranean
Parts used: mainly the peel

Details: Citrus covers a wide range of botanicals used in the making of gin including sweet and bitter orange, lemon, lime, lime leaves, grapefruit, pomelo, yuzu and kumquat and all the variations in between.

Of all the botanicals citrus is the first to emerge from the still bright and zingy, adding 'lift' to the gin. When tasting gin, if there is citrus present you will generally taste this first as it adds a top note to any gin.

The peel is most commonly used, but some gins use the whole fruit. Most of the essential oils are contained in the zest or peel. Citrus is usually added last to the still and sometimes not macerated at all but steamed in a vapour basket above the neutral grain spirit as it is heated.

Many distillers use citrus to a greater or lesser extent in their creations and citrus garnishes are tried and tested as a complement to gin and tonic.

GIN HISTORY IN SNIPPETS

THE BLACK DEATH AND GIN

Gruesome as it sounds, gin has a surprising link with the Black Death.

AD 1348–1351 ~ In AD 1348 the Black Death arrived in the Low Countries and rapidly spread to the rest of Europe. A combination of bubonic plague, caused by infected flea bites; pneumonic plague, transferred from person to person in saliva by coughing or sneezing; and septicaemic plague devasted the population of Europe. All forms of the plague caused neurological symptoms as the plague bacteria attacked the central nervous system, resulting in what was known as the *Danse Macabre* or Dance of Death.

To ward off the 'evil humours' juniper wood was burned in people's homes (to little effect). Plague doctors wore bizarre plague masks with beak-like extensions packed with herbs and juniper berries to protect them from inhaling infectious vapours from their patients. Juniper cordials or tonics were also believed to be a prophylactic against catching the plague.

It wasn't long, however, before juniper tonics stopped being medicinal and became recreational.

CHAPTER 3

HOW TO TASTE GIN
(SO EVERYONE THINKS YOU KNOW WHAT
YOU'RE TALKING ABOUT)

THE DEFINITION OF A CONNOISSEUR

Have you ever listened to someone talk about 'nosing' a gin? Or read the words of an expert pontificating about the 'mouthfeel' of a gin or how the finish was short/medium/long? And that's before they even start to talk about the nuances of key botanicals. Chances are you are in the company of a gin connoisseur.

The definition of a connoisseur is 'an expert judge in matters of taste'. And if that sounds a little daunting then take heart. You don't have to be a connoisseur to fully appreciate the kaleidoscopic flavours of gin.

All you need to fully appreciate gin is your nose, your taste buds and a little practice. By the end of this chapter, you will be if not a connoisseur then confident in your ability to judge a gin for yourself.

BEGIN AT THE BEGINNING

To start, choose a gin you like. This might seem like teaching your grandmother to suck eggs, but you will be more attentive to the following if you choose a gin you already have a fondness for.

Next, pour a small amount of your favourite gin neat into a small balloon glass. A red wine glass will also do. Make sure the gin and the glass are at room temperature.

Fat Legs vs Thin Legs

Before you begin to taste your gin give it a swirl around the glass. If the liquid clinging to the sides of your glass looks oily with big fat 'tears' running down the side then you know the gin is going to be big on flavour and packed with botanicals. A thin liquid that runs easily down the glass indicates a lighter spirit.

So: 'Fat legs' = big flavour. 'Thin legs' = lighter flavour. 'Skinny legs' = you're drinking vodka.

NOSING YOUR GIN

It's an odd thing to say, but professionals in the gin industry really do talk about nosing gin when all they really mean is sniffing it. But that doesn't sound quite so elegant, does it? Before you can properly taste gin, you have to nose it first. Like you would nose wine or whisky before you go on to taste it.

To avoid looking like a complete noseless amateur there is a right way and a wrong way to nose your gin. Forget swirling your gin round and round your glass as you would wine. Gin is a spirit and has a much higher alcohol content than wine, which is generally around 11–14% ABV. The stronger alcohol content in gin means you can't plunge straight in with a wine connoisseur's great sniff after swirling your gin round your balloon glass. To do so would anaesthetise your sense of smell.

First let the gin settle from your swirling to check out the legs of the gin. Then take a small sniff – think genteel old lady sniffs. Continue to take small sniffs and each time you sniff you will appreciate different aromas coming off the gin until you have a pretty good aroma map of your chosen gin.

A Whiff of Juniper

Ask yourself is it floral, herbal, citrus, piney, spicy? Like perfume, every gin will have its signature aroma. One that will hopefully be consistent from batch to batch. Some notes will be dominant. You may get a pungent whiff of juniper, which tells you that the gin is a juniper-forward gin (more on that later). But there will also be other notes accompanying the juniper.

Perfume is not one particular scent but a combination. And therein lies the perfumier's skill. Gin is the same. In time you will know a good gin just by nosing it.

80% of Taste is Aroma

Why is nosing gin so important? Why not just get straight in there and start tasting it? Well, 80% of what you taste is aroma. Yes, a whopping 80% of what we taste comes from smell. Your taste perception is mostly smell.

To further explain, there is something called retronasal olfaction. This means that while you are eating or drinking there are aromas emanating from your mouth, or oral cavity, which contribute to the taste of your food or drink. The aroma molecules are going in by the back door, via your throat and up into the nasal cavity. Sneaky little aroma molecules!

Sniffing, or orthonasal olfaction, does something different. The aroma molecules go straight up into your nasal cavity. Therefore, it is important to nose your gin first to distinguish between the two. Combine them together by taking a sip and you have a full flavour map of your gin.

Add in a garnish or two and you can see how difficult it gets to pinpoint those pesky flavours.

TREATING YOUR TASTE BUDS RIGHT

So retronasal olfaction is working hard. But that doesn't mean you should ignore your taste buds.

Everyone has them. Look in the bathroom mirror and stick your tongue out. See those little red bumps on your tongue? Those are your taste buds.

Imagine life without those little red bumps on your tongue. Imagine a life without the senses of taste or smell. Hard to imagine, yes? So you need to treat your taste buds right. Smoking taints and dulls your sense of taste. Similarly, eating garlic or strong spicy foods before you drink gin will also affect your sense of taste.

To best taste gin your palate needs to be neutral. And you need to be neither hungry nor full. Similarly, if you have a cold, not only will your sense of smell be affected – and remember 80% of taste is aroma – but your taste buds won't be at their most receptive.

HOW TO TASTE

Just like nosing your gin, where you don't take great sniffs, when tasting your gin you don't take a big greedy gulp. Take small sips. Think genteel old lady again, but this time sipping sherry. Try to press the gin to the roof of your palate with your tongue to get the maximum all round flavour and help with that retronasal olfaction. Try it first neat. Then add a drop of water and taste again. Just a drop mind. You don't want to dilute your gin too much.

THE BIG FIVE

There are five basic tastes that your taste buds will pick up: sweet, sour, bitter, salty and umami or savoury. Easy enough to remember if you count them on your fingers. Your first impression of a gin will be one of these five. Often a gin is predominantly one but with the addition of another. Well-made gins are quite complex – and unravelling the complexity is what makes tasting gin fun.

MOUTHFEEL

After your initial impression of which of the big five your gin is, we move on to the mouthfeel. Remember earlier we talked about the look of gin in the glass. If the gin has fat legs and looks slightly oily then it will have a big mouthfeel. If the gin has thin legs then the mouthfeel will be light.

Similarly, does it have a smooth feel? Some gins can be almost creamy. Smoothness is an indication that the gin is well made. If the gin is rough it won't be so well made. We all have at least one memory of bringing back home a bottle of duty-free spirit that tasted so good when we were on holiday on a sun-drenched beach. Only to get back home and find the same spirit made our eyes water and the back of our throat burn. Bad gin can be like that, too.

JUNIPER, JUNIPER ALL THE WAY

Once you are decided on which of the big five your gin is and you have a good idea of the mouthfeel you will start to pick up other flavours. Remember everyone's taste experience is different. So don't worry if you read that a gin is dominant in say 'asparagus' and when you taste it you can only taste 'peas' (I'm joking here, but you get the point).

Hopefully, though you will taste juniper. In fact, juniper should be the dominant flavour. Contemporary gins have pushed the boundaries of gin to its very junipery limits, almost to the point where some gins don't appear to have any juniper in them at all. But to be classed as gin the dominant flavour must be juniper.

If the juniper is particularly strong we say the gin is juniper-forward. Simply put it means the juniper makes itself quite obvious at the start of the tasting. You don't have to go looking for it.

OTHER FLAVOURS

After juniper, you will hopefully be picking up other flavours. Remember how big a part aroma plays in taste? Well, this is where it can get confusing.

For example, when someone says a gin is floral, they are really talking about the aroma. Floral is not a flavour. And most flowers are quite bitter anyway. If you don't believe me pop out to your garden and nibble on a rose petal. But it is quite difficult to separate aroma from flavour and this makes it difficult for anyone to really nail down those flavours. Ask yourself, is the gin herbal, spicy, citrusy or 'floral' as well as piney? Or is it a combination of two or more? After juniper, most gins will have another quite dominant flavour. This will be their signature botanical. You will discover in time that you get more adept at picking out these subtle nuances of flavour.

For instance, cassia bark is a good one to pick out. The strong cinnamon taste is warming and can in some gins be quite strident. If a gin has cassia bark as one of its botanicals then the distiller has included it for a reason. It lends a warm spiciness to gin and can extend the finish (see page 44). Gins with cassia bark in them tend to have more weight and punch.

THE FINISH

Finally, we come to the finish. Experts will talk about the gin having a short, medium or long finish. This just means the length of time the flavour lasts in your mouth. Does it linger or is it forgotten quite quickly? Does it leave a warming spicy impression? A citrus zing? A mellow herbal note? Floral perfumery? Or all-out juniperiness?

A QUICK TASTING CHECKLIST

Pour yourself a glass of your favourite gin and ask yourself the following questions:

- **Are the 'legs'…?**
  - Fat
  - Thin
  - Somewhere in between

- **Is the aroma…?**
  - Piney
  - Spicy
  - Citrus
  - Floral
  - Herbal

- **Can you detect any scent in particular? Vanilla or rose, for example?**

- On tasting, which of the 'big five' is most evident?
  - Sweet
  - Sour
  - Bitter
  - Salty
  - Umami

What is the mouthfeel like?
- Big
- Medium
- Light
- Smooth
- Rough

What is the strength of the juniper?
- Strong
- Medium
- Weak

What other flavours are coming through? Can you detect some of the botanicals?
- Spicy
- Citrus
- Floral
- Herbal

Is the finish…?
- Short
- Medium
- Long

CONCLUSION

So this chapter will hopefully have helped debunk some of the jargon floating about around gin and now you will feel more confident when tasting gin. Try to feel sure of your judgement at deciding if you like a particular gin or not. Remember, everyone's taste and sense of aroma is different. There are no right or wrong gins out there and it is up to you to choose which ones you would like to have in your gin cabinet.

GIN HISTORY IN SNIPPETS

DUTCH GENEVER

So who exactly invented gin as we know it? And where did it come from? The Dutch would have you believe it was they who founded the whole modern gin phenomenon. The Belgians would disagree. But all would agree that the use of juniper in medicine happily segued into a juniper-flavoured spirit some time in the fourteenth and fifteenth centuries.

1568 ~ Initially, production of genever, the forerunner of modern gin, was centred on the Low Countries with the focus on Antwerp. The Low Countries was a region encompassing modern Belgium, Holland, Luxembourg, parts of northern France and western Germany. Religious persecution by the Spanish beginning in 1568 at the start of the Eighty Years War shifted production away from Antwerp and predominantly up into the Netherlands, with wave after wave of refugee artisan distillers.

1575 ~ A family of refugees called Bulsius arrived in Amsterdam. Changing their name to Bols they established a dynasty of distillers of genever, which continues to the present day.

1602 ~ The Dutch East India Company (VOC) received their charter and access to the world's spice trade ensured the flourishing diversity of spirit production. Thanks to the VOC, Amsterdam became the centre of world trade with genever rapidly becoming one of its lucrative exports.

CHAPTER 4

10 GO-TO GINS FOR YOUR CABINET

In the words from a famous hit musical — well, sort of — these are a few of my favourite gins. I have picked ones which I hope will give a broad range to your embryonic gin cabinet. I have included some of the well-known staples as well as others you may not have heard of, or tried only in bars. They range in flavour from the delicate and sweet through to fruity, to spicy and to punchy.

I give you a little of their stories, the key botanicals, tasting notes and suggested serves. The gin serves are only guidelines. You may prefer to serve your gins differently, and please do. Experimentation is the name of the game.

You may also decide after trying one or two of the gins that they are not for you. In time you will make your own choices. And like most ginthusiasts your cabinet will probably grow.

THE COCKTAIL GIN

BEEFEATER LONDON DRY GIN

ABV: 40%

Origin: England

First produced in 1876 by James Burrough, Beefeater London Dry Gin is a British stalwart of the gin category. The distillery itself was started in Cale Street, Chelsea by the Taylor family in 1820. Bought out by Burrough in 1863 for £400 – a heck of a lot of money in those days – he soon set about producing a range of popular spirits. By 1908 the distillery had expanded into new premises on Hutton Road, Lambeth.

In 1958 Beefeater was on the move again into an old pickle factory in Kennington. And in 2005 the brand was bought out by Pernod Ricard when a revitalisation of the brand began.

Beefeater is still produced today to the original recipe by Master Distiller Desmond Payne MBE, who personally oversees the buying of the botanicals.

If you are expecting something more commercial and mass produced you might be surprised. Beefeater is currently shaking off its image of the sort of gin your grandparents might have had in their sideboard. The modern Beefeater has been bottled with a series of 'Limited Edition' bottles to make this gin look cool.

The Botanicals: Juniper, coriander seed, angelica root, angelica seed, liquorice root, orris root, almond, lemon peel and Seville orange peel.

TASTING NOTES:

The nose is light, fruity and definitely juniper with the slight sour note of a classic gin.

Beefeater is a juniper-forward gin, light on the coriander. It has a full-bodied fruity mouthfeel with a nice long citrus finish. Liquorice root adds a certain sweet spiciness. There is a faint sourness after adding a drop of water.

Perfect as a cocktail gin. It is robust enough to hold its own in a Gimlet (see page 144). In a Breakfast Martini (see page 150), its fruitness has a chance to shine. Of course, it is just as good in a G&T.

THE CONTEMPORARY GIN

DRUMSHANBO GUNPOWDER IRISH GIN

ABV: 43%

Origin: Ireland

The Shed Distillery distils gin in the small village of Drumshanbo close to the shores of Lough Allen in County Leitrim, Ireland, and is owned by P J Rigney. Patrick J Rigney is an entrepreneur with thirty plus years experience in the drinks industry. A director of The Fastnet Brands Company, he brings his vast knowledge and experience to this gin. The attention to marketing detail is everywhere, from the raised letters on the bottle to the website.

The very bottle of Drumshanbo is an experience. It has got to be one of the most distinctive gin bottles out there: a vivid ridged blue tactile bottle reminiscent of old apothecary bottles and with a label with perforated edges that completes the look. There is a cute little booklet with delicately snipped corners tied around the neck of the bottle. Even the wooden stopper doesn't escape the attention to detail, with a copper collar stamped with Gunpowder Irish Gin.

The jackalope, a North American mythical animal, a fabled cross between a jackrabbit and antelope,

has become something of a hoax in America and one wonders if by using it as the gin's logo Rigney isn't just pulling our legs a little bit.

The Botanicals: Juniper, angelica, orris, caraway, coriander, meadowsweet, cardamom, star anise, Chinese lemon, Oriental grapefruit, lime leaves and gunpowder tea.

TASTING NOTES:

On the nose subtle juniper and a hint of the spice to come.

The gin has a slight oily mouthfeel with a flavourful punch. Initially juniper and citrus with the slight green stuffiness of coriander. Then the tang of the gunpowder tea kicks in with a long finish. Star anise is there and becomes more evident with every sip.

The recommended signature serve is 40ml of Drumshanbo with 140ml of premium tonic and a wedge of fresh red grapefruit. You could also try it with a lemon wheel garnish and a star anise to complement the botanical.

I'm sure there are many different combinations out there that would work just as well. This gin is so original that it will pair up with several different tonics and each time produce something curious and extraordinary.

THE OLD TOM GIN

HAYMAN'S OLD TOM GIN

ABV: 41.4%

Origin: England

Hayman's are proud of the fact they have been a family distillery since 1863. The latest Christopher Hayman is a fourth-generation master distiller, the great-grandson of James Burrough, founder of Beefeater Gin. In 2007 they released their Old Tom Gin based on an old family recipe, sparking a revival of the Old Tom style (see page 11) among craft distillers. Their recent rebranding, like Beefeater, has brought them back to the fore of British gin.

Family recipes dating back to the first master distiller are at the heart of their distilling ethos, which includes a 'traditional' two-day distilling process with small-batch copper stills, the smallest of being only 140 litres.

The Botanicals: Juniper, coriander, angelica root, orris root, liquorice root, nutmeg, cinnamon, cassia bark, orange and lemon peels.

TASTING NOTES:

There is a sweet toffee-like juniper fragrance with citrus overtones when you nose this gin.

It tastes smooth and sweet. This is a pleasingly rounded gin with plenty of juniper and citrus. There are bold hints of liquorice and cinnamon, with a long, spicy liquorice finish. One of the best Old Tom gins out there.

Old Tom automatically suggests itself as a sipping gin, drunk neat to fully appreciate all its fine flavours.

Old Tom Gins are also the base spirit for a Tom Collins and this gin fits that cocktail perfectly. Add 60ml of Hayman's Old Tom with 30ml freshly squeezed lemon juice and 15ml sugar syrup to a shaker with ice. Shake and strain into a highball glass filled with ice. Top with club soda and garnish with an orange slice and maraschino cherry.

THE NAVY STRENGTH GIN

PLYMOUTH NAVY STRENGTH GIN

ABV: 57%

Origin: England

Plymouth Gin has a long
history. The company was
founded in 1793 and is now
the oldest distillery in the
UK that continues to
distil on its original
site. Due to its
location, Plymouth
Gin has had a
long and lucrative
association with the
Royal Navy. While
the ratings were
given rum, officers
were given gin. And
quite a lot of it. By
the mid-nineteenth
century the Royal
Navy was purchasing
1000 barrels of gin
a year.

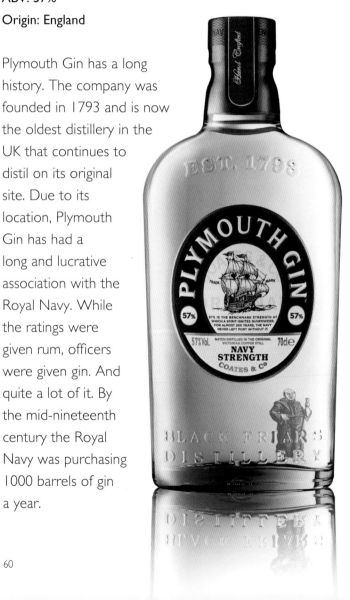

In 1993 Head Distiller at the time, Desmond Payne, reintroduced the Navy Strength to celebrate the brand's 200-year-old history. Today, a lot of gin distilleries have a Navy Strength expression as part of their category, but Plymouth Gin is synonymous with Navy Strength Gin. (Note, there is both a Plymouth Gin original at 41.2% ABV and the Navy Strength version at 57% ABV.)

The Botanicals: Juniper, coriander, angelica root, orris root, cardamom, orange peel and lemon peel.

TASTING NOTES:

On the nose is citrusy juniper with the delectable perfume of cardamom.

The taste is full-bodied, aromatic and herby with a strong juniper punch accompanied by lemon and spice.

Plymouth Gin is the perfect gin for a robust G&T. Use premium Indian tonic and garnish with lemon or lime zest.

Rather appropriately, it is also good in a Gimlet (see page 144).

THE SIPPING GIN

THE BOTANIST

ABV: 46%

Origin: Scotland

Made by Bruichladdich Distillery on the Island of Islay, mainly known for its whisky distilleries. For an island with a population of just over 3,200 people, it has no less than eight working whisky distilleries, and Bruichladdich is one of them. A Victorian distillery built in 1881 exclusively to produce whisky before declining, like so many Scottish distilleries, into disuse, it was reinvigorated by community effort and reopened in 2001 to return to the art of making whisky.

In 2011 Bruichladdich started producing gin and a whole lot of love has gone into this gin. Indeed, the man/woman hours that go into each batch, from the foraging, preparation and to what must be one of the longest distillation runs at seventeen hours, means this gin is a true labour of love. The Botanist typifies the essence of craft distilling.

Nine core botanicals are macerated for twelve hours in a Lomond pot still called 'Ugly Betty'. Then begins the slow process of distillation. The other twenty-two botanicals are distilled by vapour infusion to give The Botanist gin its distinctive lightness of flavour.

The Botanicals: The twenty-two island botanicals include:
apple mint, chamomile, creeping thistle, downy birch, elder,
gorse, hawthorn, heather, juniper, lady's bedstraw, lemon balm,
meadowsweet, mugwort, red clover, spearmint, sweet cicely, bog
myrtle, tansy, water mint, white clover, wild thyme and wood sage.

TASTING NOTES:

The fragrance of this gin is like a hay meadow in summer: complex, floral and grassy. Gentle on the juniper, it is soft and inviting.

On taste this gin delivers what it promises in the bottle and the nose. It is smooth with a medium mouthfeel, soft and sensuous. If hay meadows in summer could have a flavour this gin would be it. Initially sweet and floral, as the aroma would suggest, the juniper then comes through, but not in a bold 'here I am, look at me' kind of way. Cinnamon and cassia can just be made out to give this gin a delicate spiciness.

How to pick out the individual botanicals? Well, you can't. It is impossible to distinguish between the thirty-one botanicals. Juniper is there, of course, and cinnamon and cassia, but after that?

The finish is medium and fades away like a soft summer breeze with you wanting more. There is no lingering woody aftertaste. This gin is light on the tails.

In short, this is a delicious sipping gin.

THE FRUITY GIN

SLINGSBY RHUBARB GIN

ABV: 40%

Origin: England

Every gin cabinet should have at least one fruity gin, particularly in the summer months when long and refreshing drinks are called for. Slingsby Rhubarb Gin does just that in a no-nonsense Yorkshire kind of way.

Named after William Slingsby – who first discovered the Tewit Well in 1571 in Harrogate, which paved the way for the town to develop into the most famous of spa towns – the 'Spirit of Harrogate', the flagship for the gins, was revived in 2015 to celebrate this heritage, with the Slingsby London Dry Gin following the year after.

Incidentally, eighty-eight springs are located around Harrogate, welling up from the large aquifer, the aquifer from which Slingsby Rhubarb Gin takes its water. Several of the botanicals are sourced locally and the rhubarb which gives this gin its flavour comes from the Yorkshire 'Rhubarb Triangle'.

Slingsby Rhubarb botanicals and water are sourced from in and around Harrogate. The gin is then distilled at Langley Distillery, then brought back to Harrogate for finishing and bottling, capturing the spirit of Harrogate. The rhubarb is distilled separately from their London Dry Gin then blended post-distillation. But this doesn't detract from the fact that this is a first-class fruit gin.

Slingsby Rhubarb is contained in a big square brick of a bottle made from opaque glass, like sea glass. There are thoughtfully placed big dimples on the sides for ease of grip. To top it off it has a chunky wooden stopper. All in all, this is a colourful nice-looking bottle to have on your gin shelf.

The Botanicals: Juniper, coriander, angelica root, orris root, cassia bark, liquorice root, grapefruit. Also, locally grown: primrose, sweet cicely, nettle, milk thistle, rosehip, green and jasmine teas, and of course rhubarb.

TASTING NOTES:

On the nose unmistakeably rhubarb, almost like the chewy sweets Rhubarb & Custard.

This gin tastes like a somewhat sherbety rhubarb. Light on juniper, this will appeal to those of you who are not sure if you like gin or not. It has a light mouthfeel, but the

40% helps give it some weight otherwise this could be in danger of being one of those lightweight fruity gins of 37.5% fame who only just scrape into the spirits category by the skin of their juniper berries. The finish is long and well, rhubarby.

A delicious summery serve is rose lemonade and homemade cucumber syrup. You could go one step further and tuck in a slice of lemon, a bruised mint leaf (not too big or it will boss everything else out of the glass) and a bruised basil leaf to garnish.

THE SPICY GIN

OPIHR GIN

ABV: 40%

Origin: England

Opihr Gin, pronounced o-peer, was created by Joanne Moore, Master Distiller at the G&J Distillers in 2013. The oldest distillery in England, founded in 1761, G&J is a heavyweight in gin distilling and its marketing team pack a powerful punch, as evidenced by the quality of the bottling, the visually appealing labelling and the interactive website.

The label, featuring decorated elephants, is a nod to Kerala where the Tellicherry black pepper botanical comes from. Most Hindu temples in Kerala own elephants, which are venerated throughout India and regarded as sacred.

Named after a 'legendary region famed for its wealth and riches, which prospered during the reign of King Solomon', Opihr is fast becoming a legendary gin. And while the region's location remains something of a mystery, thankfully Opihr Gin is more of a reality. Furthermore, it's a reality inspired by the ancient Spice Route from which it sources the majority of its botanicals.

The Botanicals: Juniper from Italy, Moroccan coriander, angelica root from Germany, ginger and cardamom from India, cubeb from Indonesia, Tellicherry black pepper, cumin and grapefruit from Turkey and orange from Spain.

TASTING NOTES:

On the nose a spicy, almost sherbet-like fragrance. Following on, there is juniper, black pepper, spice and the sweet perfume of cardamom.

This is a medium-bodied gin, spicy and with a slightly sour hint due to the cubeb. Juniper holds its own and isn't submerged by the cubeb or Tellicherry black pepper. Cardamom is there, and at the finish, there is a long peppery spicy note.

Premium Indian tonic works well with this gin, at a ratio of 1:2. Try a slice of orange and fresh red chilli slice for a real kick to your serve if you are feeling brave.

THE SAVOURY GIN

GIN MARE

ABV: 42.7%

Origin: Spain

Produced in a long-standing distillery in the small fishing village of Vilanova, outside Barcelona, Gin Mare is typical of the Spanish bravery in pushing the boundaries as to gin flavours. Styled as 'pan Mediterranean', Gin Mare is a savoury gin and gathers its key botanicals from across the sea – quite aptly as the name 'mar' means 'sea' and, interestingly, also 'maternal'.

Basil from Italy, thyme from Greece, rosemary from Turkey, and Arbequina olives are the key four botanicals that give Gin Mare its unusual savoury flavour. It also uses sweet orange from Seville, bitter orange from Valencia, lemons from Lleida, and, of course, juniper (grown on the distillery land) and coriander. Each botanical is distilled separately in a barley base spirit, with the citrus in particular macerated for an extraordinarily long time.

The bottle is a thing of beauty with a sensual shape and delicate blue tinge, with a white olive leaf relief design. I have to say, though, it is awkward to pick up and a bit hefty. When pouring I have one hand round the bottle's neck and the other supporting the rest of the bottle. All this is forgiven, however, when it sits in serene maternal splendour on the shelf of my gin cabinet.

The Botanicals: Juniper, coriander, basil, thyme, rosemary, olive, sweet orange and bitter orange.

TASTING NOTES:

The nose is sweetly herbal with a lacing of juicy oranges that greets you warmly.

A full-bodied gin, savoury with a warm rounding of orange. Juniper is there. The rosemary is not dominant and the balance of sweet and savoury is good. The finish is medium with, again, that hint of orange groves.

Mediterranean tonic is the natural pairing along with a big fat juicy blood orange wheel and a sprig of rosemary. If you're feeling in a particularly savoury mood then try sprinkling cracked black pepper over the ice before pouring.

THE COMPOUND GIN

ABLEFORTH'S BATHTUB GIN

ABV: 43.3%

Origin: England

Unlike some compound gins, Ableforth's distil their gin first with botanicals in a copper pot still before taking a portion of the distillate, compounding it with a further six botanicals and then blending it back into the original distillate. A long old process, you might think. But it's one that gives Ableforth's the edge over some other 'bathtub' or compound gins out there.

The distinctive bottles wrapped in their brown paper, string and black wax further give this gin a faux rough-and-ready look that the sophisticated contents belie. The colour of the gin itself is pale straw, as you would expect from a compound gin.

The Botanicals (infused): Juniper, coriander, cassia bark, clove, cardamom and orange peel.

TASTING NOTES:

The nose is warm, spicy, citrusy juniper.

A smooth dry gin. The cardamom, clove and cassia all add a spicy, earthy depth without any one of the three pushing to the fore.

Premium Indian tonic and a wedge of orange, with a twist of orange zest to add further depth to the orangy-ness is a good serve for this gin.

THE CASK-AGED GIN

CAMPFIRE CASK AGED GIN

ABV: 43%

Origin: England

Cask-aged gins are becoming more and more popular among gin lovers. The category is expanding at quite a rate. Gin lovers are always on the lookout for something new and cask-aged gins might just be it. The tannin in the wood of the barrel, along with traces of the original contents, all add to the botanical map of the gin.

Prior to the passing of the Single Bottle Act of 1861, gin was transported out of a distillery in wooden barrels. This gave the gin colour, aroma and flavour. As the gin didn't remain in the barrel for too long but could be sold straight away, it didn't take on the stronger flavour of whisky, which has to remain in the barrel for three years and a day.

Cask- or barrel-aged gins, however, are usually only in the barrel for a few weeks, months or maybe up to a year. Campfire Cask Aged Gin, from the Puddingstone Distillery, is part of that long tradition. Rested for twenty-two days in American oak ex-bourbon casks, the gin, based around their Navy Strength recipe, takes on the soft sweet vanilla notes of bourbon, and a pale straw colour.

The Botanicals: Juniper, coriander, angelica root, orris root, rooibos, roasted hazelnut, golden berry, culinary lavender, fresh grapefruit peel and fresh orange peel.

TASTING NOTES:

On the nose there is sweet vanilla and juniper with citrus faintly in the background.

The brief allegiance with the ex-bourbon barrel produces a soft, rounded mouthfeel of vanilla and juniper, sweet and almost creamy. The vanilla doesn't dominate the gin and cause an unpleasant clash; rather it harmonises with the juniper and citrus. The finish is spicy, oaky and dry.

Try it served neat over ice diluted with ginger ale. Or treat as you would a bourbon. The signature serve, a Fireside Manhattan, uses six parts cask aged gin to one part sweet vermouth, prepared and served in the manner of a martini.

GIN HISTORY IN SNIPPETS

MADAM GENEVA: PART 1

The term 'Mother's Ruin' didn't come about until late in the nineteenth century. Its negative connotation refers to a period in gin's history in the late seventeenth and early eighteenth centuries, more commonly known as the 'Gin Craze' when Madam Geneva was the queen of London city streets.

Genever is the forerunner of modern gin. The term was anglicised to gin at the time it became popular in England and was also known as Hollands or strong water.

1688 ~ William of Orange (William III) came to the English throne and in the next year set about instigating a series of statutes, one of which was effectively to deregulate the distillation of spirits. Anyone could now become a spirit distiller by pasting a public notice to a lamp post and waiting the statutory ten days.

William didn't particularly like gin or genever but he liked the French even less. France was a major exporter of wine and brandy, so William imposed heavy duties and taxes on the importation of wine and brandy. This snubbing of France and deregulation of homemade spirits saw an increase in the consumption of spirits, essentially gin.

Gin was cheap compared to beer. Water was unclean and unsafe to drink, and disease from unhealthy drinking water was common, particularly among the poor of urban areas. This combination of unlicensed distilling, unsafe drinking water and expensive imported wine sparked a flicker of public consumption of gin that became a flame that blazed into the Gin Craze in a very short time.

1689–1726 ~ Gin consumption rose apace, particularly in London. Thousands of gin shops sprung up all over the capital. The quality of this unregulated gin was often dire; it was gin but not as we know it today. Turpentine was substituted for juniper to simulate the resinous berry at a much cheaper price. Sulphuric acid was used in distillation, which when combined with ethanol produces diethyl ether. When distilled this compound gives gin a sweetness and certain anaesthetic properties.

1730 ~ There were approximately 7000 spirit shops in London alone.

CHAPTER 5

BASIC BAR TOOLS AND GLASSES
YOU CAN BUY ANYWHERE

This chapter covers the basic barware you will need to make the perfect G&T or craft a great cocktail, including some handy equipment: jiggers and measures, shakers, strainers, bar spoons, muddlers, juicers, glassware and ice. Little extras you might need but already have in your kitchen are cocktail sticks, a blender, chopping boards and knives, a potato peeler (makes a great citrus peeler) and cute paper straws.

Bar equipment need not be expensive. You can find everything you need in your local supermarket or online and if you don't want to splash out, a lot of the equipment you already have in your kitchen will do just fine.

I have a handy drawer in my kitchen where I store almost all of the necessary equipment, apart from glasses and shakers. Whenever I'm making a G&T or a cocktail I can find what I need without going to look for it.

JIGGER AND MEASURES

If there is just one piece of equipment you do need to spend money on it is an accurate jigger. A jigger is a double-ended cup for measuring out your gin. At one end is a 25ml/.75fl oz or 30ml/1fl oz measure and at the other is a double measure, 50ml/1.75fl oz or 60ml/2fl oz. You can use either as long as you keep the ratios consistent. There are no standard measures of a single or double shot, so any cocktail recipe that doesn't give accurate measurements should be treated with caution.

I have bought quite a few jiggers and thimble measures (the single version of a jigger) in my time, only to find out they were wide of the mark when it came to accuracy. An inaccurate jigger/ measure will ruin your cocktails. It might be stating the obvious but when you measure your ingredients make sure you measure accurately. Take your time. Measure up to the mark. And unless you are a highly trained bartender – and I'm talking world class here – don't free pour. Only the most professional of bartenders can accurately measure out spirits without a jigger.

Also, it pays to spend a little more on your jigger. Browse online. There is a fantastic array of jiggers and bar equipment out there, in all colours from stainless steel to rose gold, copper and psychedelic.

The one I use is nothing fancy. Just stainless steel but with some very handy internal measurements of 15ml, 25ml and 45ml.

SHAKERS

Next on your must-have list of cocktail tools is a shaker. The majority of cocktails are shaken as opposed to stirring in a glass.

Dry shaking is when you shake your ingredients without ice. This is usually when one of your ingredients is pasteurised egg white. Effectively, you are emulsifying your egg white and combining it with the other ingredients, something that is harder to do when your shaker is filled with chunks of ice. You can also cheat and use an electric hand whisk of the kind used to froth milk. This will thoroughly emulsify your egg white and save arm ache. After dry shaking to emulsify, you then add your ice and shake again to chill your drink.

Shaking your ingredients in a shaker filled with ice does several things to your cocktail. First, and most obvious, it chills your drink. And most cocktails taste better when cold. When shaking vigorously for a minute you will notice your shaker getting very cold to the touch and water droplets from condensation forming on the outside.

Second, you are diluting your drink. This might seem like an odd thing to do, but most cocktails taste better when chilled and slightly diluted.

While you are busily shaking your cocktail shaker, tiny pieces of ice are breaking off from the chunks of ice that are bashing together in the shaker. These tiny pieces then melt to dilute your drink. Finally, you are aerating your drink and making the texture lighter.

There are many cocktail shakers out there. Again, supermarkets and online are good places to buy.

For the home cocktail-maker, a standard shaker bought in a supermarket is more than adequate for the job and there are some quite nice-looking ones around, including copper and rose-gold coloured options.

The classic shaker is one you will instantly recognise from its shape. It has three parts to it: the can (the large tumbler), the top (which has a coarse strainer built in) and the cap, which should fit on snugly.

STRAINERS

You should have at least one cocktail strainer in your gin cabinet, preferably two. Strainers are essential for filtering out any little bits of fruit or herb or ice pieces that may spoil your otherwise perfect cocktail. But at the same time, they shouldn't eliminate the 'fluffiness' of the drink that you made by shaking it.

There are two types of strainer: the Hawthorne strainer and the fine strainer. Both are useful to have for when you need to double strain your cocktail. Both can be bought online.

The Hawthorne strainer is shaped a bit like a table tennis bat with a spring around the edge. You use it by holding it in the mouth of the shaker can, where the spring then holds it in place. You pour the shaken cocktail through the strainer into your glass.

Cocktails will often call for fine straining, and some for double straining, using both, and while the Hawthorne will be adequate for most cocktails, the fine strainer really does the job much better. Shaped like a conical tea strainer you hold it over your glass and pour through it from your shaker. You can make do with a tea strainer if you don't want to go to the bother of hunting down a fine strainer. But you'll be amazed at the difference a decent strainer makes to the quality of your cocktails.

BAR SPOON

A bar spoon is basically a spoon with a long elegant twisted stem, and sometimes with a flat end. It is a useful stirring tool or can be used to create layered cocktails by pouring the ingredients down the twisted stem. In the hands of a good bartender, it is a thing of beauty, acting like a conductor's baton orchestrating a symphony of cocktails. Just watch a bartender pour tonic down the twisted stem into a copa glass of gin and ice. It is said that pouring the tonic into the glass this way keeps all the fizz.

It is also used for measuring out cocktail ingredients. The standard measurement of a bar spoon is 5ml, the same as a teaspoon. Some cheap bar spoons, like cheap jiggers, are inaccurate and not worth the little money you spend on them. Buy cheap and you end up paying double.

The flat end is supposed to be used as a muddler, but I've never found them to be fit for purpose for muddling (see page 90). And on more than one occasion I have bent the thin stem of the spoon by energetically muddling basil for a Gin Basil Smash (see page 147).

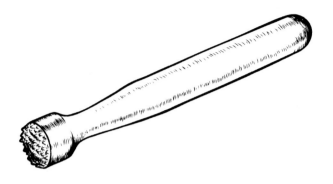

MUDDLERS

A muddler is a fun tool to have in your gin cabinet. Like a mini rolling pin with a serrated end, it's designed to crush or bruise herbs, spices and fruits in your shaker in a similar way to a pestle and mortar, to release the oils and flavours. It's essential for cocktails such as Gin Basil Smash (see page 147). Find yourself a heavy plastic one that can be cleaned using hot soapy water. The wooden ones are more difficult to keep clean and hygienic.

JUICERS

Most cocktails call for an element of sweet and sour, with the sour often freshly squeezed lemon juice. So a juicer is an essential element of your kit.

Manual ones with the long-hinged handle like the one shown here are fine. They do the job and keep hold of the pips, which is what you want. But I always seem to make quite a mess with them, squirting lemon juice all over the kitchen. If I am making a lot of cocktails I much prefer to use an electric juicer. This might seem quite an expense to splash out on, but I think it's worth it. If only to save you cleaning-up time.

If you are without, then either a fork or a good old-fashioned squeeze through your fingers will do.

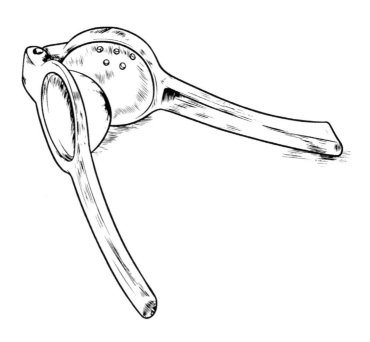

GLASSWARE

This is where you can get creative with the presentation of your drinks. There are lots of bargains to be had in stores or online. I like to rummage around charity shops for old glassware from the 1950s, 60s and 70s.

There are six basic glass styles used for gin and tonics and cocktails: the copa de balon or balloon glass, the highball (similar to a Collins glass but only a bit fatter, which makes little difference), the Martini or cocktail glass with its iconic cone shape, the coupe glass (think 70s Babycham), the squat old-fashioned glass, and the champagne flute (often used for gin fizzes if you want to look elegant).

The Copa de Balon

Copa de balon is Spanish for balloon glass and this gives you some idea of its shape. Prior to the Spanish Revolution in serving gin (that's a whole other book, by the way) gin and tonics were served in straight-up Collins or highball glasses. The copa is used for gin and tonics with room for plenty of ice and garnishes. And of course it has a stem to hold onto and avoid getting chilly fingers as with a traditional highball.

You must at least once in your life watch a
Spanish bartender whizz round large chunks of
ice in your copa to make the glass cold, drain off
any melt, then carefully place garnishes with
tweezers over your gin of choice, before pouring
tonic down the twisted bar spoon. Artistry.

The Highball and Collins

Tall and slim, the highball and Collins were the glasses of choice before the copa de balon came along and virtually elbowed them out of fashion. They still have a place though, in long cold drinks with plenty of fizz.

The Martini or Cocktail Glass

The iconic Martini glass needs no explanation. This perfect vehicle for an elegant cocktail conjures up images of black tie-clad elbows on polished wooden bars holding a Gin Martini aloft while piano music plays softly in the background.

The Coupe Glass

Also used as an alternative for a Martini, the coupe is a fine and dandy receptacle for gin cocktails that include frothy egg white.

The Old-Fashioned Glass

This is a squat, straight-sided, no-nonsense kind of glass. The old-fashioned is also known as a rocks glass and is used just for that purpose: drinks on ice.

The Champagne Flute

Prosecco flute is probably a more apt name these days, as Prosecco gin cocktails seem just the thing at summer parties.

ICE

Although not strictly barware, good-quality clear ice is as essential as any piece of equipment in your home bar.

Ice is a magical thing. It transforms your gin and tonic into a thing of beauty. I cannot stress enough the importance of good-quality clear ice to your G&T. Without it, your drink will not only look inferior but rapidly become lukewarm with the heat of the room, your hand or the sun, and the taste won't be the same – and who wants that.

Ice works by cooling your drink as it melts into it. And there is a trade-off: in order to have a cold drink that tastes good, it must suffer some dilution. Therefore it makes sense to have chunks of ice in your drink that cool slowly. Large chunks of ice will melt slower than small chunks of ice, so it pays to have large chunks filling your glass. By the time you've finished your drink, they should be no more than half melted.

Ice is also used in cocktail shakers to rapidly cool the ingredients. As the chunks of ice collide, tiny pieces break off which melt and produce that cooling effect. They also add a little bit of texture to the finished cocktail and help aerate it.

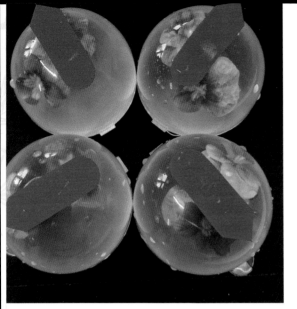

Crushed ice is used in frappe drinks such as the Bramble (see page 162). You can crush your ice in a bag by bashing with a rolling pin, an activity that is strangely therapeutic.

Buy bags of clear chunky ice in your local supermarket or freeze your own in an ice-cube tray. The silicone moulds that you can buy are quite handy. These come in a variety of shapes and sizes. Round ones are fun (see picture above) but I have to say, though, that most of the novelty ones are pretty much useless if you want to cool your drink properly. Freeze and pop out your cubes into a sturdy bag, freeze again and continue in the same way until you have a nice stock of cubes.

CHAPTER 6

WHICH MIXER WITH WHICH GIN?

Bubbles are important. They carry aroma and hence flavour. And the colder and bigger and more long-lasting they are, the more aroma and the more flavour. Mixers tend to be fizzy for that reason. That is why a simple G&T with its cold crisp fizziness is one of the most refreshing and tasty drinks around.

There are almost as many mixers on the market these days as gins, which can make it all rather confusing. If it wasn't difficult enough choosing a gin, you now have to decide how to pair it. This chapter will help you decide for yourself the best mixer to choose for your gin. At the end, there will also be a few easy-to-make cocktail syrup recipes. And, like choosing a gin, there is no right or wrong mixer to go with your gin; it's down to taste preference.

TONIC WATER

Gin and tonic go together like fish and chips. It feels like they have been around forever. Yet gin mixed with tonic water is a nineteenth-century invention, originating in India, among the British army.
The original tonic was created out of medicinal expediency. Quinine, made from cinchona bark, was administered to ward off malaria but taken in liquid

form it tasted bitter and unpalatable. Adding it to soda water, sugar and gin, thought to aid digestion, disguised its bitterness and created the forerunner of the G&T we know today. So originally a G&T was drunk for its perceived health benefits.

In 1858, Erasmus Bond, a Victorian mineral water manufacturer created his 'improved aerated tonic liquid'. In 1870, the Swiss brand Schweppes, already successfully producing soda water since 1783, followed suit, producing their first Indian Tonic Water. And you could say the rest is history. But not quite…

In 2005 a new company called Fever-Tree released a Premium Indian Tonic Water on to the mixer market, spearheading an advance of premium mixer manufacturers using natural ingredients to match the increasing diversity of craft gins. The boom in gin has in part been fuelled by these innovative mixer manufacturers. You can now pair your gin with flavours as diverse as tart Sicilian lemon to floral hibiscus. There is almost certainly a mixer out there to match your gin and your taste preference.

But don't forget the humble plain or Indian tonic. For years it has partnered gin with perfect simplicity, letting the gin shine through. And long may it continue to do so.

NAMES TO LOOK OUT FOR

This list is not exhaustive by any means but hopefully may point you in the right direction.

Fever-Tree

After the launch of their Premium Indian Tonic Water, the company went on to launch more flavours including, Mediterranean – good with savoury gins, Elderflower – goes well with floral gins – and finally Aromatic – which pairs nicely with juniper-forward gins. I say finally but the FT drinks menu is more extensive than this and includes a range of Refreshingly Light tonics with a lower calorie count.

Fentimans

Unlike Fever-Tree this company has been around for just over 100 years, but they are not a drinks dinosaur and easily rival Fever-Tree in their diversity. One tonic to mention is their Connoisseur Tonic which pairs delightfully with any gin. They also do a rather nice Pink Grapefruit flavour for citrus lovers.

Schweppes

Those who thought that the behemoth Schweppes was dead are wrong. It is still a world-class tonic water. In 2017 they launched their premium 1783 range to compete with the new mixers. The skittle or egg-shaped bottle is a nod to their past, while the new flavours such as Crisp Cucumber embrace the current trend in flavoursome tonics. Their attention to carbonation is still the same and is at the heart of their brand ethos.

Merchant's Heart

Set up in 2015, Merchant's Heart are a small premium manufacturer who make 'spirit enhancers'. Their Hibiscus flavour naturally pairs well with floral gins.

Double Dutch

A flavoursome range of mixers that can be enjoyed on their own or in cocktails.

The London Essence Company

A small range of tonics. Their Grapefruit & Rosemary pairs well with savoury gins.

SODA WATER

Soda water is fizz at its simplest: carbonated water with a small amount of sodium bicarbonate added. It's the fizz in a Tom Collins (see page 58) and often in a Gin Fizz (see page 135).

If you are not fond of its slightly salty taste you can always use sparkling mineral water instead.

SOFT DRINKS

Ginger ale pairs perfectly with some of the rhubarb gins. Think cooking. What flavours would ginger go with? It is also the fizz in the Floradora cocktail (see page 156).

Rose lemonade is very popular and rightly so. Its Turkish Delight rose flavour lifts many a gin in a summery concoction and it can be substituted for Prosecco in a Gin Fizz (see page 135).

Silician lemonade is another mixer that pairs well with gin. Good-quality Sicilian lemonade is tart without being acidic.

Plain lemonade without any bells and whistles adds a touch of sweetness to a gin for those of you who are not fond of tonic water's slight bitterness.

Cola is a surprising mixer for gin. You would normally think rum and coke or vodka and coke but

cola is sometimes paired with a robust gin and is
not too bad at all.

COCKTAIL SYRUP RECIPES

SIMPLE SYRUP

Simple syrup is just sugar pre-dissolved in water, in
the ratio of 2:1, or 1:1 if a lighter syrup is preferred,
to make it easy when you want to add a touch of
sweetness to your cocktail recipes to balance the sour
of lemon or lime.

It's as easy to make as it sounds. Simply add 2 cups of
sugar (granulated is fine) to every 1 cup of water in a pan.

Heat gently to dissolve the sugar; do not boil.
Cool slightly, then pour into a sterilised bottle. It will
keep in the fridge once cool for a few months.

For the following recipes don't be tempted to let the
sugar mixture come to the boil. Not only will this spoil
the flavour but it will alter the viscosity of the liquid.

> *Tip: It doesn't really matter which measurement you
> use to make cocktail syrups, as long as you measure by
> volume rather than weight and use the ratio of 2 sugar to
> 1 liquid. I use American cups because I find that an easy
> way to measure ingredients. 1 cup = 240ml volume.*

BLACKBERRY SYRUP

A deep jewel purple of a syrup, a drop of which will transform your G&T into something quite special. The aroma as it cooks will fill your kitchen with the smell of ripe-berried autumn. It also makes a non-alcoholic alternative to crème de mûre in the Bramble cocktail (see page 162).

Ingredients:

250g blackberries (frozen are fine for this recipe)
1 cup (240ml) water
2 cups (480ml by volume) sugar
Or 1 cup (240ml by volume) sugar for a lighter syrup

Method:

- Simmer the blackberries and water in a pan with the lid on gently for 20 minutes.
- Leave to cool in the pan and to further infuse the blackberries.
- Strain the liquid through a fine-mesh sieve into a measuring jug. You should have more than 1 cup of liquid as the blackberries will have released a lot of juice. Don't waste the blackberries (delicious with cream!).
- Measure the liquid and pour into a clean pan. Add double the volume of sugar to liquid as if you were making a simple syrup, i.e. 2 cups of sugar

for every 1 cup of liquid.

- Heat gently for 5 minutes until the sugar crystals dissolve, taking care not to let the syrup catch on the bottom of the pan.
- Bottle in a sterilised container, let cool and, then store in the fridge. It will last a few weeks.

RHUBARB SYRUP

This syrup has a delicate rhubarb flavour that infuses your gin with the essence of spring.

For this recipe, you must use forced rhubarb. Old green stems will not produce the pretty pink colour you need for the syrup and you will need considerably more sugar to sweeten them. Buy them fresh in spring when they are in season. And pick stems that are bright pink and unblemished.

Ingredients:

4 sticks rhubarb, chopped (about 400g)

1 cup (240ml) water

2 cups (480ml by volume) sugar

Or 1 cup (240ml by volume) sugar for a lighter syrup

Method:

- Place the chopped rhubarb and water in a heavy-bottomed pan, preferably non-stick. Place over a medium heat and slowly bring to simmer.

- Gently simmer for about 20 minutes until the rhubarb is very soft, taking care not to boil. Your kitchen will smell heavenly.
- Skim off any foam that appears. This won't spoil the flavour of your syrup, but it will spoil the look of it.
- Take the pan off the heat and leave to cool.
- Strain through a fine-mesh sieve by gently pressing with the back of a spoon until you have squeezed out most of the liquid. Keep the pulp – it will be delicious in a crumble or cake.
- Measure the liquid. You will need I cup of rhubarb liquid. Return to the clean pan and add the sugar and heat slowly to dissolve. There is no need to boil.
- Once the sugar has dissolved the liquid should be a lovely glossy pink. Pour through a funnel into a sterilised jar or bottle. It will keep for a few weeks in the fridge.

CUCUMBER SYRUP

Cucumber syrup makes a nice addition to a number of gins, whether fruity, herby or juniper-forward. And like the others, it is easy to make.

Ingredients:

1 cucumber, peeled

2 cups (480ml by volume) sugar

Or 1 cup (240ml by volume) sugar for a lighter syrup

Method:

- Once the cucumber is peeled, blitz it in a blender until you have cucumber mush.
- Strain the mush through a fine-mesh sieve into a jug or bowl. Press with the back of a spoon to squeeze out as much of the juice as you can.
- Sieve the liquid again but this time through a sieve lined with a muslin cloth.
- Measure the liquid which should be a pale clear green. For every cup of liquid add 2 cups sugar to a clean pan.
- Heat gently for 5 minutes, taking care not to boil the liquid.
- Cool slightly and pour into a sterilised bottle. It will last for a few weeks in the fridge.

GIN HISTORY IN SNIPPETS

OLD TOM GIN

A style of gin, sweeter than London Dry but drier than Dutch genever, forming a historic bridge between the two, Old Tom is currently seeing a resurgence in popularity.

18th to 19thC ~ The origin of Old Tom as a style of gin is elusive. It emerged at the time of the Gin Craze when gin distilling was primitive, crude and sometimes downright poisonous. One train of thought is that sugar or liquorice was added to these coarse gins to make them more palatable.

But where the name Old Tom comes from is just as elusive. One version is that following the Gin Act of 1736 a one Captain Dudley Bradstreet set up a gin shop called the Puss & Mew. In the window of his shop, he hung the sign of a cat. There was a slot under the cat's paw where money could be fed. The gin would then be poured through a pipe by Bradstreet straight into the waiting client's mouth.

Though the existence of Bradstreet's gin shop is undisputed, this doesn't explain why a style of gin should be named after a particular gin shop. After all, there were approximately 7000 gin shops in London at the time.

Another version of the origin of the name is that an old tomcat fell into a vat of gin. This is not particularly believable, as the gin afterwards would have been undrinkable.

The final version of the name's origin and the most credible comes from a distillery. Hodges' Distillery had a young apprentice named Tom Norris. The Master Distiller was also called Thomas. Young Tom, after finishing his apprenticeship, opened a gin shop in Covent Garden selling a gin called, you guessed it – Old Tom, in homage to his old master.

Wherever the name came from it stuck to the style of gin like sugar syrup. Wooden plaques shaped like black cats were hung outside gin shops and public houses in the eighteenth and nineteenth centuries to advertise that they were selling Old Tom.

20th to 21stC ~ The twentieth century saw a demise in the popularity of Old Tom gin until 2007, when Hayman's released their gin using an old family recipe. This sparked a revival in Old Tom among craft distillers which happily continues today. Now if you want to sample Old Tom there is a whole gin cabinet to choose from.

Strawberry Rose

This is a slightly more fiddly garnish to create than the previous one. You need a steady hand, a sharp paring knife, a little patience and a strawberry, of course.

Make four incisions in the strawberry down the four 'sides'. It helps if you chill the strawberry in the fridge first. It will firm up and keep its shape, making cutting easier.

Then, in between the first four cuts, make four more incisions downwards.

Finally, carve out a small hole in the centre and gently turn back the petals of the rose without breaking them.

Chilli Flower

Take one small red or green chilli, a bowl of iced water and a paring knife and in a few minutes you will have a pretty chilli flower to put in your G&T ~ if you dare.

Flamed Lemon Twist

This lemon twist can be achieved without flaming it. But flaming citrus zest brings out a whole other dimension of flavour. Using metal tongs gently hold the strip of zest over a naked flame for a few seconds only. Then twist round a chop stick or similar and hold until the lemon twist 'sets'. Use a couple of pegs to make this easier.

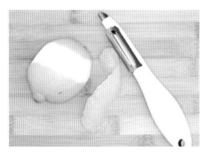

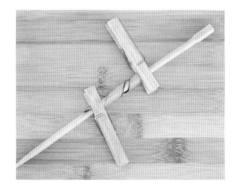

Lime Leaf

A cute easy to carve leaf shape out of a strip of lime zest. Just peg it to your cocktail glass.

Orange Zest and Rosemary Sprig

This lovely combination goes a treat in savoury gins.

Cucumber Dahlia

Ok, so you might not want to fiddle around making
a cucumber dahlia to put in your G&T when a simple
slice of cucumber is so much easier and tastes the
same. But do it, just once, for fun.

   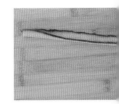

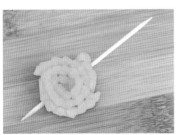  

GIN HISTORY IN SNIPPETS

PROHIBITION AND GIN

Prohibition gave gin drinkers two things: bathtub gin and some great cocktails.

1920–1933 ~ The United States was under the constitutional ban on the production, importation, transportation and sale of any alcoholic beverage whatsoever, enforced by the Volstead Act, formally the National Prohibition Act. Many years of campaigning by the Temperance Movement and social pressure groups spearheaded by the umbrella organisation the Anti-Saloon League culminated in a general state ban on a substance believed to be corrupting the nation, both politically and personally.

1920 ~ The derogatory term 'bathtub' for homemade gin first appeared in 1920. Bathtub in the north of America and 'moonshine' in the south, both homemade alcohols, flourished during the Prohibition Era, which saw an increase in sales of small portable stills.

There is some confusion as to the exact origin of the term. It could have come about because the bottles used were too tall to be filled from a kitchen faucet and therefore had to be filled from a bathtub tap. It could also originate from the making of gin itself in the metal bathtubs of the day – ideal vessels for making and hiding the spirit in plain sight of the authorities. Who would suspect a bathtub of being part of a bootlegger's alcohol production line?

Either way, as mentioned earlier, bathtub gin had a pretty poor reputation at the time. Made using poor-quality, illegally distilled alcohol or worse, redistilled denatured alcohol, it was mixed with juniper oil and glycerine to sweeten. The result was often dire and frequently fatal: 50,000 deaths in the Prohibition Era are attributed to illegal alcohol.

Bathtub gin lives on today in some excellent examples of the craft and has shaken off its negative connotations. And thankfully its lethal properties.

Another side of Prohibition was the sudden loss of employment for bartenders. While illicit speakeasies were happy to serve up bathtub gin and moonshine liquor of dubious origin, many bartenders were used to serving more upper class and discerning clientele. A great number of bartenders therefore emigrated in droves to London, Paris and Havana, fostering a boom in cocktail culture in these cities. Such bartenders were the DJs of their time and had quasi-star status.

Harry Craddock, one such émigré, came to London to work as Head Bartender at the American Bar at The Savoy. His seminal work, *The Savoy Cocktail Book*, with its 750 cocktail recipes, is still highly regarded today. Quite the showman, rumour has it that he shook the last cocktail on the eve of the Prohibition Era.

1933 ~ The Eighteenth Amendment to the constitution in January 1920 described above was repealed on 5 December 1933. But not after America had experienced thirteen long 'dry' years. However, it was drier for some than others. While private consumption of alcohol continued with the wealthy simply stockpiling their supplies before Prohibition was put into force, public consumption was much more affected. Alcohol consumption went down, while the health of the nation improved.

Although Prohibition was never completely effective it did have an impact on American bars, with the speakeasy replacing the saloon. Bootlegging became an alternative source of income for some. Prohibition was big business, worth US$2,000 million to bootleggers and organised criminals like Bugs Moran and Al Capone.

CHAPTER 8

MASTER 10 EASY CLASSIC
GIN COCKTAILS

Making cocktails need not be as difficult as it may seem. You don't have to be an expert mixologist creating infusions and foams and smoke and whatnot to make some quite delicious cocktails. Often the most delightful are the classics that have proved their popularity over time. These are also the easiest to make with just a few ingredients.

You can find most of your ingredients in the supermarket or online. Have fun creating something new, and in the same way you would choose a gin, let your taste buds decide which cocktails you like.

The measurements used in the recipes are metric. Use the handy table below if you need to convert metric millilitres to imperial fluid ounces:

ml	fl oz
5	$\frac{1}{6}$
7.5	$\frac{1}{4}$
10	$\frac{1}{3}$
15	$\frac{1}{2}$
20	$\frac{2}{3}$
25	$\frac{4}{5}$
30	1
45	$1\frac{1}{2}$
50	$1\frac{3}{4}$
60	2

GIN FIZZ

The Gin Fizz is the easiest cocktail you will ever make. There are lots of gin fizzes out there, most famously the Ramos Gin Fizz, a monument to creamy fizziness with nine separate ingredients. But essentially a gin fizz is just gin and something fizzy, traditionally soda water. Nowadays you can almost add anything fizzy to your gin to call it a gin fizz. A popular style at the moment is to add Prosecco to gin. If you add a little cocktail syrup, this can become quite a sophisticated summer drink.

Some recipes call for pasteurised egg white to ramp up its creaminess, but this is optional and the traditional fizz does without.

Tip:

Use your favourite craft gin and have fun experimenting with different flavour combinations by adding some of the cocktail syrups mentioned in Chapter 6.

If you don't have a shaker don't worry. You can just as easily make a simple gin fizz using a jigger to measure your gin. And if you don't have a jigger or measure to hand, go freestyle! This really is the most forgiving of cocktails.

Equipment:

Shaker, jigger, lemon squeezer, Hawthorne strainer, flute or highball glass

Ingredients:

- 50ml your favourite gin
- 25ml freshly squeezed lemon juice
- 15ml simple syrup (see page 111)
- soda water or something fizzy, to top up
- lemon slice, twist or wedge, to garnish

Method:

- Shake the first three ingredients in a shaker with ice then strain into a flute or highball glass.
- If using a highball glass fill it with ice first, but this isn't necessary for a flute glass where it would look odd. If 25ml of lemon juice is too sour for you then just reduce the amount until you are happy with your fizz. But remember, your fizz should have an element of refreshing citrus.
- Top up with soda water and garnish with lemon slice, twist or wedge.

GIN MARTINI

From the easiest of cocktails to make to the one
that I think is the hardest. On the face of it, the
Gin Martini should be an easy cocktail to make,
with only two or three ingredients, starting with gin
and vermouth. But a really good Martini requires
precision and care.

There are many stories about the birth of this
most iconic of cocktails. One is that it was created
by legendary barman 'Professor' Jerry Thomas.
Thomas claimed to have invented it at San
Francisco's Occidental Hotel.

Rather romantic is the story that it was created
during the 1800s gold rush in Martinez California.
The legend is that a gold miner who had struck
it rich wanted to celebrate in a local bar. As they
didn't have champagne the bartender concocted a
drink from gin, vermouth, bitters, maraschino liqueur
and a slice of lemon. And so the Martinez was born,
which later became the Martini.

A more prosaic version is that the Martini brand
of sweet vermouth, first produced in 1863, gave rise
to a concoction of gin and vermouth, abbreviated to
Martini. Presumably by drinkers in a hurry.

Whatever the origin of the Gin Martini cocktail,
it is one cool drink and a perfect aperitif as the

sun goes down. Even the cone-shaped glass it is served in has understated iconic status. Truly, if ever a cocktail deserved an accolade it is the Martini.

Okay, so it is almost impossible to write this without mentioning James Bond. Whereas 007 preferred his Martinis shaken, many purists will argue that this causes unnecessary dilution and should be avoided at all costs. At the moment the stirred contingent are holding sway. But it may only be a matter of time before shaken becomes the thing again. Time will tell.

One thing everyone agrees on is that your cocktail should be cold. Whether you are shaking or stirring, you must use ice that is fresh out of the freezer, as dry as possible. And if you can, chill your glass in the freezer, too.

Tip:

Choose a gin you like. This might seem obvious, but the character of your gin will determine the character of your final drink. There's no hiding place in this cocktail for a cheap budget gin.

THE MARTINI 5 WAYS

Equipment:

Shaker (optional), bar spoon, jigger, Hawthorne strainer, fine strainer, lemon peeler, Martini or cocktail glass

THE DRY MARTINI ~ 5:1 RATIO

Ingredients:

- 50ml London Dry Gin
- 10ml extra dry vermouth
- twist of lemon, lime or orange peel, to garnish

Method:

- Stir both ingredients with your bar spoon in a shaker with ice. Try not to break up the ice.
- Hawthorne strain into a chilled cocktail glass and garnish with a twist of lemon, lime or orange peel, depending on the character of your gin.

Variations on the Dry

Naked ~ with the barest smidgen of vermouth
Wet ~ a ratio of 3:1
Extra wet ~ a ratio of 1:1.

THE DIRTY MARTINI ~ 5:1 RATIO

Ingredients:

- 50ml London Dry Gin
- 5ml or 1 bar spoon dry vermouth
- 5ml or 1 bar spoon olive brine from a jar of good olives
- olive, to garnish

Follow the same method as for the Dry Martini, adding the olive brine to the shaker, but double straining. Garnish with an olive on a cocktail stick.

THE FILTHY MARTINI ~ 5:1 RATIO

Ingredients:

- 50ml London Dry Gin
- 5ml dry vermouth
- 2.5ml or ½ bar spoon fresh lime juice
- 2.5ml or ½ bar spoon olive brine
- olives and a lemon twist, to garnish

Follow the same method as for the Dry Martini, adding lime juice and olive brine to the shaker, but double straining. Garnish with olives and a lemon twist.

THE GIBSON MARTINI

Garnish a Dry Martini with a small cocktail onion (yes really) to make a Gibson.

THE PERFECT MARTINI

Make as Dry Martini but with 50% dry + 50% sweet vermouth.

GIMLET

In the gin sour category, the Gimlet has a sweet,
tart, sharpness about it that makes a refreshing
summer drink on a hot day. Pale and interesting in a
Martini glass with a simple lime wheel for garnish, it
looks great: subtle and understated.

Made with 5 parts gin to 1 part lime syrup. Rose's
Lime Juice Cordial is traditionally used. The Gimlet
is the simplest of cocktails to make. But don't let its
simplicity fool you. You will still need to take care in
preparing it to avoid a sickly sweet mess.

Established in 1867 by Lauchlan Rose, Rose's
Lime Cordial was originally devised to preserve
lime juice with sugar rather than the more
traditional rum. It was given to sailors to combat
scurvy or vitamin C deficiency. Rose imported
limes from the West Indies to the docks in Leith,
Scotland and on to his factory in Commercial
Street. With the Royal Navy also based in Scotland
at Leith, Rose had a ready customer. His lime cordial
industry boomed and can claim to be the first
manufacturer of a concentrated fruit drink. Today
the cordial is made by the Coca-Cola company and
is still going strong.

Equipment:

Shaker, jigger, Hawthorne strainer, fine strainer, lime squeezer, Martini or cocktail glass

Ingredients:

- 50ml London Dry Gin
- 10ml lime syrup or Rose's Lime Juice Cordial
- lime wheel, to garnish

Method:

- Add both ingredients to a shaker with ice. Shake vigorously.
- Double strain through a Hawthorne strainer and fine strainer into a chilled Martini glass to catch any small pieces of ice.
- Garnish with a lime wheel.

GIN BASIL SMASH

Perfect in summer using fresh basil, the Gin Basil Smash is a relatively new cocktail, an infant in the world of mixology. Created July 2008 by Joerg Meyer, owner and bartender of the Lion Bar de Paris in Hamburg, this is his signature cocktail and was originally called Gin Pesto. It won an award for the Best New Cocktail at The Tales of the Cocktail Spirited Awards in July 2008.

Tip:

Don't use your best, most expensive gin. Traditionally, Hendrick's gin is used for this cocktail, but as the flavour of the basil does dominate, any good-quality gin will do.

Equipment:

Shaker, muddler, jigger, Hawthorne strainer, fine strainer, lemon squeezer, any glass you fancy.

Ingredients:

- 10–12 fresh basil leaves, plus extra to garnish
- 60ml London Dry Gin
- 25ml freshly squeezed lemon juice
- 15ml simple syrup (see page 111)
- fresh basil leaves, to garnish

Method:

- Muddle (see page 90) the basil leaves with the lemon juice in the shaker. Give them a real bashing.
- Add the rest of the ingredients and some ice to the shaker. Shake vigorously.
- Fill a glass with ice. Double strain the smash into the ice-filled glass through a Hawthorne strainer and fine strainer to catch any green bits.
- Garnish with fresh basil leaves.

VARIATION: GIN CILANTRO SMASH

The Basil Smash lends itself to lots of variations. Try substituting cilantro leaves (coriander) for the basil. While not as pretty a vivid green as the Gin Basil Smash, the result is nevertheless rather delicious with a fresh greenness and slight spiciness.

Ingredients:

- A handful of cilantro (coriander) leaves
- 60ml London Dry Gin
- 20ml freshly squeezed Silician blood orange juice
- 5ml freshly squeezed lime juice
- 15ml simple syrup (see page 111)

Method:

- As for Gin Basil Smash. Garnish with cilantro/ coriander leaves.

BREAKFAST MARTINI

The signature cocktail of celebrated bartender
Salvatore Calabrese, 'The Maestro', the Breakfast
Martini is a modern classic and a cousin of the Gin
Martini.

One morning in 1996, while enjoying his toast
and marmalade at breakfast, it struck him that
marmalade would make a delicious addition to a
cocktail. At the time he was working at the Library
Bar at The Lanesborough Hotel in London.

The Breakfast Martini is in good company. Harry
Craddock's 1930 *The Savoy Cocktail Book* also
mentions a marmalade cocktail. And Salvatore has
inspired other bartenders to create their own sweet
concoctions based on preserves.

The Breakfast Martini is a sweet cocktail with a
sharp edge from the lemon. A great marmalade
cocktail. Utterly delectable and good at any time of
the day.

Tip:

*Beefeater is a good gin to use as it has a fruity flavour
without being dominant and remains true to its juniper
roots.*

Equipment:

Shaker, bar spoon, jigger, Hawthorne strainer, fine strainer, lemon squeezer, peeler, Martini or cocktail glass

Ingredients:

- 50ml London Dry Gin
- 15ml triple sec
- 15ml fresh squeezed lemon juice
- 1 bar spoon of orange marmalade
- a twist or shredded orange peel and a triangle of toast, to garnish

Method:

- Dry shake all the ingredients. Add ice to the shaker and shake again.
- Double strain through a Hawthorne strainer and fine strainer into a Martini glass.
- Garnish with shredded orange peel and add a triangle of toast for authenticity.

WHITE LADY

This cocktail is a gin classic whose origins are as cloudy as the drink. Two Harrys can lay claim to being the creators of this citrus colossus in the world of cocktails.

Harry one is the Harry Craddock of the 1930s *The Savoy Cocktail Club* book fame, in which he printed a recipe of this creation. Note, however, that printing a recipe does not warrant creatorship over the cocktail.

Harry two is Harry MacElhone. He is said to have originally used crème de menthe in the recipe before wisely switching to gin when he opened his own bar, Harry's New York Bar, in Paris.

Both Harrys are contemporaries, so either is possible.

Equipment:

Shaker, jigger, Hawthorne strainer, fine strainer, lemon squeezer, peeler, coupe glass

Ingredients:

- 50ml London Dry Gin
- 20ml triple sec
- 10ml freshly squeezed lemon juice
- 10ml simple syrup (page 111)
- 15ml pasteurised egg white
- orange peel, to garnish

Tip:

If you find the dry shaking difficult in this particular recipe, you can cheat by using a mini electric whisk of the kind you would use to froth milk. In this case, I think it's perfectly acceptable.

Method:

- Add all the ingredients to a cocktail shaker and dry shake very vigorously for about a minute. You want the egg white to emulsify with the other ingredients.
- Add ice to the shaker and give it a good hard shake to chill your cocktail.
- Double strain through Hawthorne and fine strainers into a coupe glass. Garnish with orange peel in as fancy a way possible.

FLORADORA

A Broadway smash of a cocktail, the Floradora is an intriguing combination of raspberry and ginger flavours. It was originally devised at the turn of the twentieth century for a chorus girl – one of the 'Florodora' girls in a successful West End musical comedy that ran for 455 performances and half a century in London. It later transferred to Broadway where it was an even greater success, with over 500 performances. And for a time the Floradora was similarly popular in the bars of New York.

The unashamedly pink and girly Floradora cocktail, which faded from the limelight towards the end of the century, is now currently experiencing a long overdue revival. Easy to make, even without a cocktail shaker (you can just stir in the ingredients), it manages to be both sweet and spicy. The sweetness of the raspberry is offset by the spicy heat of the ginger ale and is an unusual combination. Normally you would partner rhubarb with ginger, but here raspberry is the unexpected yin to ginger's yang. Use a ginger ale with real bite for a definite kick. You can garnish with raspberry and a wedge of lime, but a sprig of mint takes the garnish to another level.

Gently bruise the leaves of the mint before placing in
the cocktail. The aroma of the mint will fool the brain
into thinking you are drinking something minty, adding
another layer of flavour to the cocktail.

Equipment:

Shaker, jigger, Hawthorn strainer, lime squeezer,
highball glass

Ingredients:

- 50ml gin
- 25ml raspberry syrup
- 25ml freshly squeezed lime juice (approx. I lime)
- ginger ale, to top up
- mint, to garnish

Method:

- Add the gin, raspberry syrup and lime juice
  to a cocktail shaker. Dry shake then add ice.
  Shake again.

- Strain through a Hawthorne strainer into a highball glass filled with ice.
- Top up with good-quality ginger ale. Garnish with mint.

NEGRONI

This love it or hate it brilliantly vermillion, bitterly herbaceous, uncompromising Italian cocktail is currently enjoying something of a revival. The Negroni is an acquired taste. If you are not used to bitter aperitifs it may come as something of a shock. Campari is the culprit. The gin and vermouth are there to soften the blow. The Negroni is a drink you will love or loathe, sometimes at the same time in equal measure.

Like a lot of cocktails, its origin is hazy. It differs from the Americano only by the substitution of gin for soda water. And as such it is purported to have come about when Count Camillo Negroni asked bartender Fosco Scarselli to pep up his favourite aperitif at the Caffè Casoni in Florence, Italy in 1919. An alternative version of its history is that another Count de Negroni invented the drink in Senegal in 1857.

Whatever the origin, the Negroni family didn't hang about and capitalised on its popularity by

founding the Negroni Distillery in Treviso, where they made ready-made versions of the cocktail.

Now at 100 years old, this venerable cocktail is listed as one of The Unforgettables on the list of the International Bartenders Association official cocktails. And it truly is an unforgettable gin cocktail, once tasted, never forgotten. You will learn to love its bitterness.

Tip:

If you really find this too bitter, try adding a splash of lemonade. It will transform the Negroni – just don't tell anyone.

Try not to use your special craft gin unless it's particularly robust. It will be bullied out by the Campari. It must be a good-quality gin, though.

Equipment:

Jigger, bar spoon, peeler, old-fashioned glass

Ingredients:

- 30ml London Dry Gin
- 30ml Campari
- 30ml sweet red vermouth.
- twist of orange peel, to garnish

Method:

- Add all three ingredients to an old-fashioned glass packed with ice.
- Stir with a bar spoon. This is one of those cocktails that should not be shaken. The tiny shards of ice that would inevitably get mixed into the cocktail will alter the mouthfeel of the finished drink.
- Add a twist of orange peel. And that's it.

BRAMBLE

A riff on a gin sour, this cocktail is evocative of autumn. Created in 1984 by the innovative Dick Bradsell when he was working as Head Bartender at Fred's Club in Soho, the Bramble is redolent of the season of 'mists and mellow fruitfulness'. Not surprising then that it was born out of the inventor's nostalgia for a childhood spent picking blackberries from damp hedgerows on the Isle of Wight.

Although he was responsible for many of the neo-classic cocktails of the 1980s and 90s, including the Espresso Martini, Dick's favourite was said to be the Bramble.

ABOUT THE AUTHOR

 Sue Telford is a Norfolk-based writer, gin blogger and cocktail photographer with a love of craft gin, cocktails and fresh flavours. In 2017, inspired by the craft gin revolution, she bought a tiny 4L air still, got herself licensed by HMRC, and effectively turned her little 9ft by 9ft kitchen into a weekend gin distillery where she set about distilling with enthusiasm.

At the time she knew nothing about distilling, although she was a keen cook in the kitchen and loved experimenting with flavours. She quickly learned through a lot of trial and error and internet research. And she is still learning.

Her cocktail photographs with their distinctive style have been featured by gin distillers.

You can find Sue Telford on her website For the Love of Gin where you will find reviews, cocktail recipes and general gin stuff. Seek her out on social: Pinterest, Instagram and Facebook.

- 4theloveofgin
- @4theloveofgin
- 4theloveofgin
- Fortheloveofgin

Find out more about RedDoor Press and sign up to our newsletter to hear about our **latest releases, author events,** exciting **competitions** and more at

reddoorpress.co.uk

YOU CAN ALSO FOLLOW US:

 @RedDoorBooks

 Facebook.com/RedDoorPress

 @RedDoorBooks

ACKNOWLEDGEMENTS

I owe a large gin and tonic to each and all of my family and friends who have put up with my endless gin talk for the last two years. I would particularly like to thank my partner Hein for his support and enthusiasm in collaborating in experiments with my little still.

Thanks should also go to Amy Traynor, Moody Mixologist, for her inspirational cocktail photographs. Her kindness and encouragement should not go unremarked. She can be found on Instagram and her website moodymixologist.com.

Jonathan and Alison Redding of Norfolk Gin have been immensely supportive at times when I wasn't sure I was a writer of gin books at all. They also know how to throw a good gin party.

My best friend Karen Devany needs a mention for her lifelong friendship and for our regular trips to hunt out old glassware and for convincing me that I was indeed a writer.

Thanks also to Heather Boisseau of RedDoor; Joey Everett for his line illustrations; Sheer Design for the fabulous book design and to all the gin distillers and mixer companies mentioned in the book who gave their time and patience.